Help Is Here for Facing Fear!

Written by
Molly Wigand

Illustrated by
R. W. Alley

ONE
CARING
PLACE

Abbey Press
St. Meinrad, IN 47577

For my Mom,
Millie Wigand,
who is one brave lady.

Text © 2000 Molly Wigand
Illustrations © 2000 St. Meinrad Archabbey
Published by One Caring Place
Abbey Press
St. Meinrad, Indiana 47577

Library of Congress Catalog Number
00-103685

ISBN 978-0-87029-344-3

Printed in the United States of America

A Message to Parents, Teachers, and Other Caring Adults

Fear and worry have always been part of the human experience. When we were young, we all experienced childhood fears. We wondered what frightening forces lurked in the night. We worried about death—for ourselves and our loved ones. Some of us feared dogs, some dreaded bathtub drains, and others lived in terror of the vacuum cleaner. These fears, though silly to grown-ups, were real to us.

The fearful aspects of our own growing-up years may seem tame compared to the realities experienced by children today. Yet children's emotional needs remain the same. Children need to express their anxieties and have their feelings validated by parents, teachers, and friends. Children need the courage to examine their fears and the skills to cope with day-to-day stress. For these important learning tasks and many others, children need caring adults to show the way.

We have a responsibility to equip young people with the psychological and spiritual tools to find a haven of security in an uncertain world. Through word and example, we need to share with our children the healing powers of communication, loving reassurance, and faith.

Our job as parents, educators, and guides is to teach children in our care to transform fears and worries into confidence and optimism. By encouraging little ones to express their fears and guiding them through the uncertainties of these complicated times, we help them find the safe and beautiful places in their lives.

Children deserve the opportunity to experience their world as a friendly place in which to learn and grow. May this book empower them to find their courage and face their fears.

—*Molly Wigand*

Everybody's Afraid Sometimes

Being human means having many different feelings. Sometimes we're happy. Sometimes we're sad. Sometimes we're friendly. Sometimes we're angry. Sometimes we're very brave. And sometimes we're afraid.

When you're a kid, lots of things can seem scary. The world can seem big and loud and dark and confusing.

Grown-ups have fears, too. Movie stars and presidents, football players and ballet dancers, teachers and coaches—everyone in the world is afraid once in awhile. But guess what? We can get the help we need to get past our fears and worries.

What Does Fear Feel Like?

When you're afraid, your body does weird things. Your palms may get sweaty. Your heart may beat really fast. You might even get a stomachache or a headache. Fear can make you feel dizzy or shaky. It might be hard to breathe. Fear can even make your hands and feet tingle. These are all normal human feelings, and everybody has them at certain times.

When you feel this way, talk to a parent or grown-up friend. Sharing your fears can make you feel safer and help your fears to fade away.

Are You Afraid of the Dark?

Your imagination can make you feel scared at nighttime. Shadows look creepy. Noises seem spooky. You may be afraid something is hiding under the bed. It might seem like monsters are in your closet.

Maybe you and your mom or dad could bake a special batch of "courage cookies" for an evening snack. You might want to ask your parents if they were scared of the dark when they were little—and what made them feel less afraid. Let your parents help you look under the bed and search the closets. Pretend that your favorite teddy bear will protect you as you sleep.

And when you say your bedtime prayers, remember that God is right there with you and will stay with you through the night.

What's Real and What's Pretend?

Some movies, TV shows, and books can make you feel scared. It's easy to get mixed up about what's real and what's pretend. The scary things you see or read during the day can make you have bad dreams or scary thoughts at night. Let your family help you choose books and movies that aren't scary.

If a TV show or book does scare you, don't keep your fears inside. Let a grown-up know. Together, try to fill your house with peaceful, happy feelings. Laughter works wonders to chase fears away.

The Whole World in God's Hands

It's scary to hear about bad things that happen in the world—like tornadoes, earthquakes, and wars.

But God's love is like an umbrella that can protect us from fear. Even when bad things happen, God's love is there. And even when we feel afraid, the world is still a beautiful place.

When you're scared or worried, think about the family and friends who love you. Enjoy the colors and sounds of nature. Think about all the good things in your life.

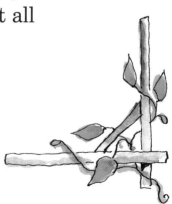

If Other Kids Tease You

Have you ever been called a "chicken" or a "fraidy cat"? It's no fun to be teased about your fears.

Remember—we're all brave in different ways. One person may be afraid of deep water, but very brave about going to the dentist. Maybe you're afraid of big, barking dogs, but you aren't scared of monsters at all.

You have a right to all your feelings, even your fears. You're doing your best and being as brave as you can. That's all anyone can expect. Ask some grown-ups how they handled teasing when they were kids. Would their ideas work for you?

One Day at a Time

Sometimes people worry about things that haven't even happened yet. You may worry you'll forget your homework. Or you might be afraid you'll get lost on your way to school.

Worrying about tomorrow takes the fun out of today. Look for the good things in every day. God gives you the courage you need to get through this day. Nobody knows exactly what will happen tomorrow, but God will always watch over and care for you.

Draw a Picture! Write a Story!

Your fears may look and feel less scary when you put them on paper.

If you're afraid of monsters, draw a picture of a scary creature. Can you find something silly about the monster? Draw a picture of yourself next to the monster. Show that you and the monster are friends.

Is bedtime scary for you? Write a story about a special, happy nighttime land. Tell how the moon and stars smile down on you and give you happy dreams.

What stories and pictures can you make to help you with your own special fears?

Life and Death

Death is a part of life. Flowers, birds, trees, and people all have their time to be born, their time to live, and their time to die. But, since nobody really knows what death is like, it can be scary to think about.

If you have fears about death, talk to a parent or grown-up friend. Many people believe death is the beginning of a brand-new life in a beautiful place called "heaven."

Always remember how much your family and friends love you. Love is the very best thing for making fears and worries go away.

Learning to Relax

You can learn to relax your body and your mind. Ask your mom or dad to help you practice. Pretty soon you'll be doing it all by yourself!

First, find a quiet place. Close your eyes and breathe slowly in and out. Feel your heartbeat calming down. Keep breathing slowly.

Now, think of your favorite place in the world. It might be your bedroom, or the kitchen, or the neighborhood playground. Imagine yourself smiling and feeling peaceful in your special place. Imagine your favorite people all around you. Imagine God protecting you with an umbrella of love.

Remember this place. Come back to it whenever you feel afraid.

Give Yourself a Pep Talk

You can learn to face your fears and worries by talking to yourself! Maybe you're afraid to ride an escalator. Here's what you might say: "Look at that big escalator. Look at all those people riding it. Nobody tripped when they got on or off. I'll bet some of those people were afraid of escalators when they were kids. And now they can ride without being scared. I bet I can ride the escalator, too."

What if you're afraid about a spelling test at school? About jumping off the diving board? Practice talking to yourself about your fears. Tell yourself that you can do it, and you will!

Stop to think about some of the fears you had when you were younger. Be proud of yourself for getting over those fears!

Facing Your Fears

Learning more about the things you fear makes you less afraid.

If you're afraid of dogs, read some books about them. Go to a pet shop and ask to hold a playful little puppy. Visit a friend who has a nice dog. Pretty soon you'll learn that dogs can be gentle and loving. You may even end up with a dog as a friend!

Maybe you feel scared when you're asked to read out loud at school. Try practicing at home. First read out loud to yourself. Then read into a tape recorder. Next, read for a parent. Then read for some friends. Before long, reading at school won't seem scary at all.

When Life Is Scary

If someone at school or home or in your neighborhood makes you feel afraid, tell a grown-up you trust. Kids should not have to keep scary secrets.

If your family or friends are having some problems that worry you, talk with your mom or dad. They love you and can help you to understand what's going on.

Sometimes parents need extra help to help you. They may take you to a "counselor," who has special training to talk with kids about their feelings. You have lots of caring people on your side!

School
Counselor

It's Okay to Feel Afraid

Just like happiness, sadness, or anger, fear is a very normal feeling. Fear is good for us when it keeps us out of danger. But fear hurts us when it stops us from enjoying our lives.

Every fear you face helps you to grow stronger and braver. When you're afraid, remember: Talk about it with someone you trust. Learn to relax and find a safe place inside yourself. Fill your mind with happy thoughts. Trust God to take care of you.

As you become more and more fear-free, you'll find it easier to find the smiles and fun in every day!

Molly Wigand is a writer and editor who lives with her husband and three children in Lenexa, Kansas. She is the author of ten children's books and has taught creative writing to children and adults. She is a frequent contributor to One Caring Place publications.

R. W. Alley is the illustrator for the popular Abbey Press adult series of Elf-help books, as well as an illustrator and writer of children's books. He lives in Barrington, Rhode Island, with his wife, daughter, and son. See a wide variety of his works at: www.rwalley.com.